HADOOP ECOSYSTEM
APACHE PIG AND APACHE HIVE
AMAZON ELASTIC MAPREDUCE
CLOUDERA QUICKSTART VM

IMPLEMENTING BIG DATA ANALYTICS USING HADOOP

AJIT SINGH

Preface

Most of the organizations are using big data for better decision making, growth opportunities, and competitive advantages. Research is ongoing to understand the applications of big data in diverse domains such as e-Commerce, Healthcare, Education, Science and Research, Retail, Geoscience, Energy and Business.

As the significance of creating value from big data grows, technologies to address big data are evolving at a rapid pace. Specific technologies are emerging to deal with challenges such as capture, storage, processing, analytics, visualization, and security of big data. Apache Hadoop is a framework to deal with big data which is based on distributed computing concepts.

The Apache Hadoop framework has Hadoop Distributed File System (HDFS) and Hadoop MapReduce at its core. There are a number of big data tools built around Hadoop which together form the 'Hadoop Ecosystem.' Two popular big data analytical platforms built around Hadoop framework are Apache Pig and Apache Hive. Pig is a platform where large data sets can be analyzed using a data flow language, Pig Latin. Hive enables big data analysis using an SQL-like language called HiveQL. The purpose of this book is to explore big data analytics using Hadoop. It focuses on Hadoop's core components and supporting analytical tools Pig and Hive.

The ultimate objective of this book is to help you become a professional in the field of Big Data and Hadoop and ensuring you have enough skills to work in an industrial environment and solve real world problems to come up with solutions that make a difference to this world. I tried at my best to explain the understanding on how a component in the Hadoop ecosystem works, why it works that way and how it fits into the design of the overall Hadoop framework.

This book explains the Hadoop framework, followed by data analysis using MapReduce, Hive and Pig on sample use cases. Big data analysis using Amazon Elastic MapReduce (Hadoop on Amazon cloud) is also explained in detail.

It also focuses on the Hadoop architecture as well as explains the Hadoop setup using Cloudera QuickStart VM. Further, MapReduce is also explained using a data analytics use case. In addition of the above, it also explains Apache Pig and Apache Hive respectively and show how these technologies can be used for solving data analysis problems as well as big data analytics using Amazon Web Services (AWS).

CONTENTS

CHAPTER 1

Introduction Big Data And Analytics

Data is growing at a rate we never imagined. Large volumes of digital data are generated at a rapid rate by sources like social media sites, mobile phones, sensors, web servers, multimedia, medical devices and satellites, leading to a data explosion. The importance of capturing this data and creating value out of it has become more important than ever in every sector of the world economy. While the potential of creating meaningful insights out of big data in various domains like Business, Health Care, Public Sector Administration, Retail and Manufacturing are being studied, data science related technologies are expanding to capture, store and analyze big data efficiently.

What is Data?
The quantities, characters, or symbols on which operations are performed by a computer, which may be stored and transmitted in the form of electrical signals and recorded on magnetic, optical, or mechanical recording media.

What is Big Data?
Big Data is also data but with a huge size. Big Data is a term used to describe a collection of data that is huge in size and yet growing exponentially with time. In short such data is so large and complex that none of the traditional data management tools are able to store it or process it efficiently.

Examples Of Big Data
Following are some the examples of Big Data-

- The New York Stock Exchange as well as Indian Stock Exchange generates about one terabyte of new trade data per day.

- Social Media - The statistic shows that 500+terabytes of new data get ingested into the databases of social media site Facebook, every day. This data is mainly generated in terms of photo and video uploads, message exchanges, putting comments etc.

- A single Jet engine can generate 10+terabytes of data in 30 minutes of flight time. With many thousand flights per day, generation of data reaches up to many Petabytes.

Types Of Big Data

BigData' could be found in three forms:

- **Structured**
- **Unstructured**
- **Semi-structured**

Structured

Any data that can be stored, accessed and processed in the form of fixed format is termed as a 'structured' data. Over the period of time, talent in computer science has achieved greater success in developing 7techniques for working with such kind of data (where the format is well known in advance) and also deriving value out of it. However, nowadays, we are foreseeing issues when a size of such data grows to a huge extent, typical sizes are being in the rage of multiple zettabytes.

Examples Of Structured Data

An 'Employee' table in a database is an example of Structured Data

Unstructured

Any data with unknown form or the structure is classified as unstructured data. In addition to the size being huge, un-structured data poses multiple challenges in terms of its processing for deriving value out of it. A typical example of unstructured data is a heterogeneous data source containing a combination of simple text files, images, videos etc. Now day organizations have wealth of data available with them but unfortunately, they don't know how to derive value out of it since this data is in its raw form or unstructured format.

Examples Of Un-structured Data

The output returned by 'Google Search'

Semi-structured

Semi-structured data can contain both the forms of data. We can see semi-structured data as a structured in form but it is actually not defined with e.g. a table definition in relational DBMS. Example of semi-structured data is a data represented in an XML file.

Examples Of Semi-structured Data

Personal data stored in an XML file

```
<rec><name>Prashant Rao
</name><sex>Male</sex><a
ge>35</age></rec>
<rec><name>Seema R.</nam
e><sex>Female</sex><age>
41</age></rec>
<rec><name>Satish Mane</
name><sex>Male</sex><age
>29</age></rec>
<rec><name>Subrato Roy</
name><sex>Male</sex><age
>26</age></rec>
<rec><name>Jeremiah J.</
name><sex>Male</sex><age
>35</age></rec>
```

can apply analytics and get significant value from it. But even in the 1950s, decades before anyone uttered the term "big data," businesses were using basic analytics (essentially numbers in a spreadsheet that were manually examined) to uncover insights and trends.

The new benefits that big data analytics brings to the table, however, are speed and efficiency. Whereas a few years ago a business would have gathered information, run analytics and unearthed information that could be used for future decisions, today that business can identify insights for immediate decisions. The ability to work faster – and stay agile – gives organizations a competitive edge they didn't have before.

Why is big data analytics important?

Big data analytics helps organizations harness their data and use it to identify new opportunities. That, in turn, leads to smarter business moves, more efficient operations, higher profits and happier customers. In his report Big Data in Big Companies, IIA Director of Research Tom Davenport interviewed more than 50 businesses to understand how they used big data. He found they got value in the following ways:

- Cost reduction. Big data technologies such as Hadoop and cloud-based analytics bring significant cost advantages when it comes to storing large amounts of data – plus they can identify more efficient ways of doing business.
- Faster, better decision making. With the speed of Hadoop and in-memory analytics, combined with the ability to analyze new sources of data, businesses are able to analyze information immediately – and make decisions based on what they've learned.
- New products and services. With the ability to gauge customer needs and satisfaction through analytics comes the power to give customers what they want. Davenport points out that with big data analytics, more companies are creating new products to meet customers' needs.

How it works and key technologies

There's no single technology that encompasses big data analytics. Of course, there's advanced analytics that can be applied to big data, but in reality several types of technology work together to help you get the most value from your information. Here are the biggest players:

- Machine Learning. Machine learning, a specific subset of AI that trains a machine how to learn, makes it possible to quickly and automatically produce models that can analyze bigger, more complex data and deliver faster, more accurate results – even on a very large scale. And by building precise models, an organization has a better chance of identifying profitable opportunities – or avoiding unknown risks.

- Data management. Data needs to be high quality and well-governed before it can be reliably analyzed. With data constantly flowing in and out of an organization, it's important to establish repeatable processes to build and maintain standards for data quality. Once data is reliable, organizations should establish a master data management program that gets the entire enterprise on the same page.

- Data mining. Data mining technology helps you examine large amounts of data to discover patterns in the data – and this information can be used for further analysis to help answer complex business questions. With data mining software, you can sift through all the chaotic and repetitive noise in data, pinpoint what's relevant, use that information to assess likely outcomes, and then accelerate the pace of making informed decisions.

- Hadoop. This open source software framework can store large amounts of data and run applications on clusters of commodity hardware. It has become a key technology to doing business due to the constant increase of data volumes and varieties, and its distributed computing model processes big data fast. An additional benefit is that Hadoop's open source framework is free and uses commodity hardware to store large quantities of data.

- In-memory analytics. By analyzing data from system memory (instead of from your hard disk drive), you can derive immediate insights from your data and act on them quickly. This technology is able to remove data prep and analytical processing latencies to test new scenarios and create models; it's not only an easy way for organizations to stay agile and make better business decisions, it also enables them to run iterative and interactive analytics scenarios.

- Predictive analytics. Predictive analytics technology uses data, statistical algorithms and machine-learning techniques to identify the likelihood of future outcomes based on historical data. It's all about providing a best assessment on what will happen in the future, so organizations can feel more confident that they're making the best possible business decision. Some of the most common applications of predictive analytics include fraud detection, risk, operations and marketing.

- Text mining. With text mining technology, you can analyze text data from the web, comment fields, books and other text-based sources to uncover insights you hadn't noticed before. Text mining uses machine learning or natural language processing technology to comb through documents – emails, blogs, Twitter feeds, surveys, competitive intelligence and more – to help you analyze large amounts of information and discover new topics and term relationships.

There are various tools in Data Analytics that can be successfully deployed in order to parse data and derive valuable insights out of it. The computational and data-handling challenges that are faced at scale mean that the tools need to be specifically able to work with such kinds of data.

The advent of big data changed analytics forever, thanks to the inability of the traditional data handling tools like relational database management systems to work with big data in its varied forms. Data warehouses also could not handle data that is of extremely big size.

The era of big data drastically changed the requirements for extracting meaning from business data. In the world of relational databases, administrators easily generated reports on data contents for business use, but these provided little or no broad business intelligence. It was for that, they employed data warehouses. But, data warehouses too generally could not handle the scale of big data, cost-effectively.

While data warehouses are certainly a relevant form of Data Analytics, the term 'Data Analytics' is slowly acquiring a specific subtext related to the challenge of analyzing data of massive volume, variety, and velocity.

Types of Data Analytics

- Prescriptive Analytics: This is the type of analytics that talks about an analysis based on the rules and recommendations in order to prescribe a certain analytical path for the organization.
- Predictive Analytics: Predictive analytics ensures that the path is predicted for the future course of action.
- Diagnostic Analytics: This is about looking into the past and determining why a certain thing happened. This type of analytics usually revolves around working

on a dashboard.

- Descriptive Analytics: In descriptive analytics, you work based on the incoming data and for the mining of it you deploy analytics and come up with a description based on the data.

Companies Using Data Analytics

Today, regardless of the industry type, there is rapid deployment of various analytical tools and technologies. It could be the tools for parsing data or the easy-to-understand visualization tools which are used for making sense of the data. Further in this blog, some of the industries that are using Data Analytics tools are discussed.

There are digital-first enterprises for whom data analytical tools are the most important weapons in their arsenal. For example, Amazon, Facebook, Google, and Microsoft cannot survive without the use of Data Analytics. Amazon widely deploys analytics in order to recommend you the right product based on the product that you bought in the past. They also make use of data in order to build customer profiles to serve them better. This way, they can provide a very customized experience to their customers.

A company like Facebook will deploy Data Analytics to find out what its users are talking about so that it can understand what products and services the users would be interested in. Since it works on ads, it needs to know the pulse of its users by making sure that the ads are up to date in terms of customization and other aspects.

Google is sitting on the mother lode of all data. They serve a few billion searches every day making it one of the most data-intensive companies on planet Earth. Due to this, the need for analytical tools at Google is inevitable. Google is also hiring the maximum number of Data Scientists.

CHAPTER 2

HADOOP ARCHITECTURE & ECOSYSTEM

Apache Hadoop is an open-source framework which allows distributed storage and processing of large volumes of structured or unstructured data across clusters of commodity hardware.

2.1 INTRODUCTION

Apache Hadoop is an open source software framework used to develop data processing applications which are executed in a distributed computing environment.

Applications built using HADOOP are run on large data sets distributed across clusters of commodity computers. Commodity computers are cheap and widely available. These are mainly useful for achieving greater computational power at low cost.

Similar to data residing in a local file system of a personal computer system, in Hadoop, data resides in a distributed file system which is called as a Hadoop Distributed File system. The processing model is based on 'Data Locality' concept wherein computational logic is sent to cluster nodes(server) containing data. This computational logic is nothing, but a compiled version of a program written in a high-level language such as Java. Such a program, processes data stored in Hadoop HDFS.

Hadoop EcoSystem and Components

Apache Hadoop consists of two sub-projects –

Hadoop MapReduce: MapReduce is a computational model and software framework for writing applications which are run on Hadoop. These MapReduce programs are capable of processing enormous data in parallel on large clusters of computation nodes.

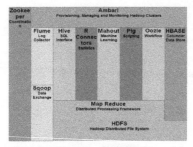

Figure 1.0 Hadoop Ecosystem (Self Drawn)

HDFS (Hadoop Distributed File System): HDFS takes care of the storage part of Hadoop applications. MapReduce applications consume data from HDFS. HDFS creates multiple replicas of data blocks and distributes them on compute nodes in a cluster. This distribution enables reliable and extremely rapid computations.

Although Hadoop is best known for MapReduce and its distributed file system- HDFS, the term is also used for a family of related projects that fall under the umbrella of distributed computing and large-scale data processing. Other Hadoop-related projects at Apache include are Hive, HBase, Mahout, Sqoop, Flume, and ZooKeeper.

One of the early big data problems was faced by web search engines where millions of web pages had to be indexed in a fraction of second in a cost-effective way. Hadoop was created by Doug Cutting and originated in Apache Nutch, a web search engine project initiated by Doug Cutting and Mike Cafarella [1].

Apache Lucene, a text search engine library created by Doug Cutting. Nutch's implementation of distributed file system and MapReduce were inspired by Google's white papers [2] distributed file system (GFS) and MapReduce [3] respectively, which described the distributed file system and distributed computing architecture Google used for intensive data processing needs. Nutch's distributed file system and MapReduce implementations were moved to Apache Hadoop as an independent subproject of Apache Lucene in 2006 to build a generic framework to solve various big data problems.

14

One of the main design features of Hadoop is its high scalability in data storage and processing capability that can be achieved by adding more nodes to the cluster. It also enables cost effectiveness as it does not demand high-end servers, instead using inexpensive commodity machines. Since it uses ordinary hardware which fails more often than high-end machines, data is replicated for fault tolerance.

Hadoop use cases are vast and cover almost all sectors of the world economy like Politics, Data Storage, Financial Services, Health Care, Human Sciences, Telecoms, Travel, Energy, Retail and Logistics [4]. For example, use of big data and cloud computing using Amazon Web Services for election campaigns played an important role in Team Obama's win in the 2012 U.S. presidential election. In the financial domain, banks use Hadoop solutions for maintaining data accuracy and compliance with regulations, and this was more complex and time consuming before Hadoop. In health care, it is used for storage, processing and analysis of millions of medical records and claims, and for capturing and analyzing massive volumes of medical sensor data. In Telecom, large volumes of mobile call records can be stored and processed in real time. In energy, insights on household energy usage can be made by processing large volumes of energy usage data and potential energy saving plans can be derived. A list of companies using Hadoop and the related use cases can be found at Hadoop wiki [5].

2.2 HADOOP ARCHITECTURE

Hadoop's underlying principle is distributed data storage and computation. Data transfer speed of hard drives is not growing proportionally with storage capacities, which slows down read and write operations. One feasible solution to this is distributed computing, where data is distributed over multiple disks and data is read and written in parallel. Since failure of one disk should not result in data loss, data must be replicated. Hadoop's file system, called Hadoop Distributed File System (HDFS), is based on this principle. When data is distributed, it's processing needs to be done in a distributed fashion. Hadoop's MapReduce framework takes care of this. In MapReduce programming model, the processing is done in two steps: in 'Map' phase, data is processed locally and in 'Reduce' phase, the results are consolidated. This also makes use of the principle that moving computation closer to data is cheaper than moving data closer to computation, especially when the size of the dataset is huge.

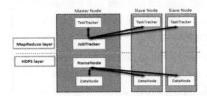

Figure 1.1 Hadoop Architecture (Self Drawn)

High Level Hadoop Architecture

Hadoop has a Master-Slave Architecture for data storage and distributed data processing using MapReduce and HDFS methods.

- NameNode:

NameNode represented every files and directory which is used in the namespace

- DataNode:

DataNode helps you to manage the state of an HDFS node and allows you to interacts with the blocks

- MasterNode:

The master node allows you to conduct parallel processing of data using Hadoop MapReduce.

- Slave node:

The slave nodes are the additional machines in the Hadoop cluster which allows you to store data to conduct complex calculations. Moreover, all the slave node comes with Task Tracker and a DataNode. This allows you to synchronize the processes with the NameNode and Job Tracker respectively.

In Hadoop, master or slave system can be set up in the cloud or on-premise

Features Of 'Hadoop'
• Suitable for Big Data Analysis

As Big Data tends to be distributed and unstructured in nature, HADOOP clusters are best suited for analysis of Big Data. Since it is processing logic (not the actual data) that flows to the computing nodes, less network bandwidth is consumed. This concept is called as data locality concept which helps increase the efficiency of Hadoop based applications.

• Scalability

HADOOP clusters can easily be scaled to any extent by adding additional cluster nodes and thus allows for the growth of Big Data. Also, scaling does not require modifications to application logic.

• Fault Tolerance

HADOOP ecosystem has a provision to replicate the input data on to other cluster nodes. That way, in the event of a cluster node failure, data processing can still proceed by using data stored on another cluster node.

Network Topology In Hadoop
Topology (Arrangment) of the network, affects the performance of the Hadoop cluster when the size of the Hadoop cluster grows. In addition to the performance, one also needs to care about the high availability and handling of failures. In order to achieve this Hadoop, cluster formation makes use of network topology.

Typically, network bandwidth is an important factor to consider while forming any network. However, as measuring bandwidth could be difficult, in Hadoop, a network is represented as a tree and distance between nodes of this tree (number of hops) is considered as an important factor in the formation of Hadoop cluster. Here, the distance between two nodes is equal to sum of their distance to their closest common ancestor.

Hadoop cluster consists of a data center, the rack and the node which actually executes jobs. Here, data center consists of racks and rack consists of nodes. Network bandwidth available to processes varies depending upon the location of the processes. That is, the bandwidth available becomes lesser as we go away from-

- Processes on the same node
- Different nodes on the same rack
- Nodes on different racks of the same data center
- Nodes in different data centers

HDFS and MapReduce layers in Hadoop 2.x are shown below. The data storage layer consists of a NodeManager (one per cluster) and DataNodes (one per slave node). The data computation layer consists of a ResourceManager (one per cluster) and NodeManagers (one per slave node). These components are explained in detail in the coming sections.

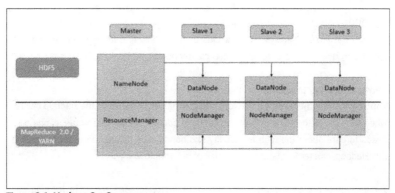

Figure 2.1. Hadoop 2.x Components

2.2.1 Hadoop Distributed File System (HDFS)

In HDFS [6] [7], files are split into blocks. The default block size is 128 MB in Hadoop 2.x generation. (In Hadoop 1.x, it was 64 MB). In a filesystem, a block is the minimum size of data that can be read or written from disk. Each block of data is replicated by a replication factor which has a default value of three and then stored on data nodes. Both block size and replication factor are configurable per file.

2.2.1.1 NameNode and DataNode

HDFS follows master-slave architecture. A cluster consists of a NameNode (master) and a set of DataNodes (slaves). NameNode and DataNodes are Java processes running on master and slave machines, respectively. Master is usually a server-grade machine and slaves are commodity machines. NameNode stores the file system metadata in persistent mode and controls file access by clients. File system metadata is stored persistently in FsImage file on NameNode's local disk. EditLog logs changes made to the file system metadata (such as creation of new files, changing file replication factor, etc.) and is also stored persistently on the NameNode's local disk. When the NameNode starts, it loads the FsImage into RAM and applies the transactions from the EditLog. It then creates a new persistent FsImage file creating a checkpoint. The old EditLog is cleared at this point.

The data blocks are stored on DataNodes. These service data read and write operations of data blocks from clients. DataNode periodically sends its block list to NameNode and NameNode stores blocks to DataNode mapping in memory.

An HDFS cluster may span multiple racks in the same or different data centers. Data centers may exist in geographically different locations. Determining on which nodes the replicas are to be placed is important in HDFS, since write operations on a remote rack are more expensive than those on local racks. HDFS follows the following replica placement policy by default: The first replica is placed on the same node as the client node. If the client is outside the cluster, a random node is chosen. The second and third replicas are placed on different nodes on a rack other than the first one. The remaining replicas are placed on random nodes and no single node should contain more than one replica and no single rack should contain more than two replicas.

2.2.1.2 FILE WRITE IN HDFS

The sequence of steps in a file write operation in HDFS is explained below [8].

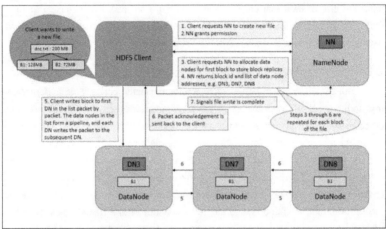

Figure 2.2. File Write in HDFS

1. Client requests NameNode to create a new file.

2. NameNode checks for client permission and duplicates and grants a lease for writing the file.

3. Client requests a list of data nodes to store block replicas.

4. NameNode returns a unique block id and a list of data node addresses.

5. The DataNodes form a pipeline and data is pushed as a sequence of packets. Client writes the packets to the first DataNode and each DataNode forwards it to the subsequent one in the pipeline. Along with the data, the checksum for each block is also sent to the DataNodes and gets stored in a metadata file.

6. For each received packet, an acknowledgement is sent back.

2.2.1.3   FILE READ IN HDFS

The sequence of steps in a file read operation in HDFS is explained below [8].

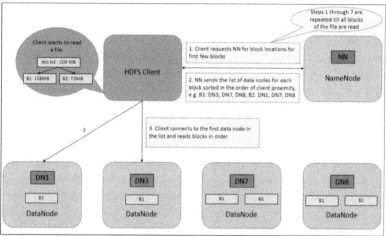

Figure 2.3. File Read in HDFS

1. Client requests the NameNode for the list of DataNodes where replicas are stored for each block of the file.

2. NameNode sends back the list of DataNode addresses sorted in the order of their distance from the client.

3. Client contacts the first DataNode in the list for each block and reads all the blocks in order. Along with the data, the block's checksum is also sent to the client and client calculates the checksum for the read data and checks if it is corrupted. If a read fails for a DataNode (DataNode is unavailable or data is corrupted), client goes to the next

4. DataNode in the list for block replica. The failed DataNodes will not be contacted for further block reads.

2.2.2 MapReduce

MapReduce [9] is a programming framework for distributed processing of large data sets on a cluster of computers. A MapReduce program typically consists of Map tasks and Reduce tasks. The initial input is split into smaller chunks called InputSplits, and processed by Map tasks in parallel. The output of Map tasks are then processed by Reduce tasks to produce the final output. The execution and monitoring of the tasks are handled by the framework itself. The framework typically schedules tasks local to the data and also handles re-execution of failed tasks.

InputFormat represents the input format for a MapReduce job. Default InputFormat is TextInputFormat. InputSplit represents the data to be processed by an individual Mapper. Default InputSplit is FileSplit. Default behavior of InputFormat is to split the input into byte-oriented logical input splits based on total input size with file system block size (default 128 MB in Hadoop 2.x) as the upper bound. The InputSplit is passed to a RecordReader which converts the byte-oriented input splits into record-oriented input splits. RecordReader reads InputSplit and generates <key, value> pairs. TextInputFormat uses LineRecordReader by default which returns a <key, value> pair with the key as the offset in file and value as the line.

One Mapper task is assigned for each InputSplit. Mapper takes input key-value pairs and transforms them into a set of intermediate key-value pairs. The transformation is performed by a map() method which is called for each key/value pair in the InputSplit. Intermediate outputs from Mapper are sorted and partitioned across the Reducers available. In the shuffle and sort step of the Reducer, relevant partitions are fetched and grouped based on the same key. In the reduce step of the Reducer, on each <key, (list of values)> pair in the input, reduce() method is called to produce the final output. Sometimes a Combiner is used which acts a local Reducer, which locally aggregates intermediate outputs from Mappers, thus reducing the data transfer from Mapper to Reducer.

MapReduce framework is illustrated by the word count example below:

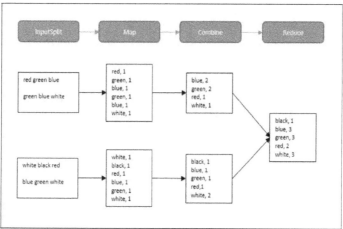

Figure 2.4. Example to Illustrate How MapReduce Works

There are two Mappers above which take each InputSplit and process it. Input to the map() function is each line and its offset in the file. The line is split into words and the intermediate outputs (<word>, 1) are generated. The combiner function which also runs locally to the Mapper, combines the count for the same word in the Mapper output. Finally, output is generated by a single Reducer where outputs from different combiners are fetched, sorted based on the key and processed to find the total count per word.

2.2.2.1 YARN / MRv2

MapReduce in Hadoop 2.x is called MapReduce 2.0 (MRv2) or YARN (Yet Another Resource Negotiator) [10]. MapReduce 1.0, the MapReduce in Hadoop 1.x, underwent many architectural changes in Hadoop 2.x.

Per-cluster ResourceManager manages resources across the cluster. Per-application ApplicationMaster is responsible for the individual MapReduce job execution and monitoring. It coordinates the Map and Reduce tasks for each MapReduce application. Per-node NodeManager is responsible for launching and monitoring the containers running in each node and reporting their status back to the ResourceManager. Containers run ApplicationMaster and MapReduce tasks with certain allocated computation resources.

2.2.2.2 STEPS IN MAPREDUCE JOB EXECUTION

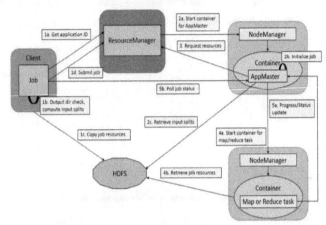

Figure 2.5. Steps in MapReduce Job Execution [8] [11]

1. Job Submission

   1.1. Client asks for an application ID from the ResourceManager.

   1.2. Check if output directory is specified and does not already exist. Checks input files are specified and calculates input splits.

   1.3. Copy resources like job jar file, configuration file and input splits to HDFS.

   1.4. Submit the job to ResourceManager.

2. Job Initialization

   2.1. ResourceManager's scheduler allocates container for ApplicationMaster and starts the container by contacting the NodeManager.

   2.2. ApplicationMaster initializes the job by creating the objects required for job progress tracking.

   2.3. ApplicationMaster retrieves the input splits from filesystem and creates map task for each input split. It also creates the required number of reducer tasks.

3. Task Assignment

   ApplicationMaster requests resources for map and reduce tasks to

24

ResourceManager's scheduler. Scheduler tries to allocate map task on nodes where the data (input split) is already stored.

Task Execution

4.1. ApplicationMaster contacts the NodeManagers and asks to start the containers for map and reduce tasks.

4.2. Resources are retrieved from the filesystems.

Map/Reduce tasks are executed.

5. Job Progression and Completion

5.1. Map and reduce tasks send the progress (how much data is processed), status (running, completed, failed) updates and a set of counter values to the ApplicationMaster every three seconds. Thus ApplicationMaster gets notified when the job is finished.

5.2. Client polls ApplicationMaster for job status and learns when job is finished.

CHAPTER 3
SET UP SINGLE-NODE HADOOP CLUSTER USING CLOUDERA QUICKSTART VM

Specialized Hadoop vendors such as Cloudera, HortonWorks, and MapR provide data management and analytical platforms packaged around Apache Hadoop. Commercialized Hadoop solutions are also available from well-known enterprises like Microsoft (Microsoft HDInsight on Microsoft cloud (Microsoft Azure), IBM (IBM BigInsights on IBM cloud (IBM SmartCloud), Amazon (Amazon Elastic MapReduce (EMR) on Amazon cloud (Amazon Web Services (AWS)). A complete list of companies who provide products that include Apache Hadoop or derivative works and commercial support can be found in Hadoop wiki [12]. The enterprise users make use of the support and services provided by these vendors to avoid complications related to Hadoop setup and maintenance and to solve their business challenges more efficiently. Cloudera's Hadoop distribution [13], CDH (Cloudera Distribution Including Apache Hadoop), comes in many flavors. Cloudera QuickStart VM provides a single-node Hadoop cluster setup and makes it easy for beginners to gain hands-on experience on Hadoop from their local machines.

3.1 SET UP CLOUDERA QUICKSTART VM

Below are the system requirements:

- 64-bit host OS
- Player 4.x or higher (Windows) or Fusion 4.x or higher (Mac)

• Minimum RAM requirement is 4GB. Allocate more memory for larger workloads. Follow below steps to install Cloudera QuickStart VM:

1. Download VMware Player [14].

2. Download QuickStart VM from Cloudera web site for VMware format [15]. (Downloads are available for VMware, KVM, and VirtualBox formats as Zip archives.)

3. Unzip the package. (Cloudera recommends using 7-Zip to extract files)

4. Open VMware Player and click on 'Open a Virtual Machine'. Browse to the extracted folder and select the file cloudera-quickstart-vm-<version>-vmware.vmx (VMware virtual machine configuration file). Cloudera VM will be

listed as below.

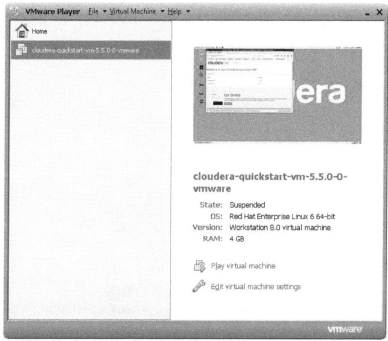

Figure 3.1. Cloudera VM Listed in VMware Player

5. Select the VM and click on 'Play virtual machine'. (If Virtualization Support is not enabled on your Windows host machine, related errors may pop up. This can be solved by enabling Virtualization Technology in BIOS setting.) The VM runs CentOS 6.4. The VM starts and the user is automatically logged in as the cloudera user (both username and password are 'cloudera'). A browser opens up as below with useful links to various Hadoop tools on the Bookmarks bar.

Figure 3.2. Browser in the Cloudera VM with Bookmark Links

6. Open Terminal and go to /usr/bin. Hadoop, Pig, Hive, HBase, Sqoop, Flume etc. are installed under the directories with the respective names.

3.1.1 HADOOP Configuration Files

The configuration files can be found under etc/Hadoop directory in Hadoop installation

directory.

Figure 3.3. Hadoop Configuration Files

- hadoop-env.sh
- Environment settings for Hadoop scripts found in bin directory of Hadoop distribution
- core-site.xml

28

- Settings common to HDFS and MapReduce

- hdfs-site.xml

- Configurations for NameNode and DataNode

- yarn-site.xml

- Configurations for ResourceManager and NodeManager

- mapred-site.xml

- Configurations for MapReduce Applications and MapReduce JobHistory Server

3.2 RUNNING WORDCOUNT EXAMPLE

Hadoop distribution comes with MapReduce examples jar file which has a number of example MapReduce programs. We will see how to execute the wordcount program from this jar. The word count problem was explained in section 2.2.2 and the same sample data is used here.

1. To display all the programs available within hadoop-mapreduce-examples.jar:

```
$ cd /usr/lib/hadoop-mapreduce
$ hadoop jar hadoop-mapreduce-examples.jar
```

2. Create input files for the wordcount program. Create files input1.txt and input2.txt on Desktop.

```
[cloudera@quickstart ~]$ cat /home/cloudera/Desktop/input1.txt red green blue
blue green white

[cloudera@quickstart ~]$ cat /home/cloudera/Desktop/input2.txt white black red
blue green white
```

3. Copy the input files to HDFS. Create an input folder under /user/cloudera/in and copy the input files.

```
[cloudera@quickstart ~]$ $ hdfs dfs -mkdir /user/cloudera/in

[cloudera@quickstart ~]$ $ hdfs dfs -copyFromLocal /home/cloudera/Desktop/input1.txt /user/cloudera/in

[cloudera@quickstart ~]$ $ hdfs dfs -copyFromLocal /home/cloudera/Desktop/input2.txt /user/cloudera/in

[cloudera@quickstart ~]$ hdfs dfs -ls /user/cloudera/in
Found 2 items
-rw-r--r--          1 cloudera cloudera                    32 2015-12-29  22:50
/user/cloudera/in/input1.txt
-rw-r--r--          1 cloudera cloudera                    33 2015-12-29  22:51
/user/cloudera/in/input2.txt
```

Note: The user can interact with HDFS using HDFS shell, which can be invoked by *hdfs dfs <command> <args>*. 'args' are file path URIs. URI format is *scheme://authority/path*. If the scheme and authority are not specified, the default values from configuration will be used. For example, *hdfs://host/path* and */path* are identical, if the configuration is set to point to *hdfs://host/*. [16]

4. Run wordcount program. Make sure the output folder does not exist already.

[cloudera@quickstart ~]$ hadoop jar hadoop-mapreduce-examples.jar wordcount /user/cloudera/in/input /user/cloudera/output

Figure 3.4. Running wordcount Program

```
                cloudera@quickstart:/usr/lib/hadoop-mapreduce
File  Edit  View  Search  Terminal  Help
    Job Counters
        Launched map tasks=2
        Launched reduce tasks=1
        Data-local map tasks=2
        Total time spent by all maps in occupied slots (ms)=31417
        Total time spent by all reduces in occupied slots (ms)=6670
        Total time spent by all map tasks (ms)=31417
        Total time spent by all reduce tasks (ms)=6670
        Total vcore-seconds taken by all map tasks=31417
        Total vcore-seconds taken by all reduce tasks=6670
        Total megabyte-seconds taken by all map tasks=32171008
        Total megabyte-seconds taken by all reduce tasks=6830080
    Map-Reduce Framework
        Map input records=4
        Map output records=12
        Map output bytes=113
        Map output materialized bytes=114
        Input split bytes=240
        Combine input records=12
        Combine output records=9
        Reduce input groups=5
        Reduce shuffle bytes=114
        Reduce input records=9
        Reduce output records=5
        Spilled Records=18
        Shuffled Maps =2
        Failed Shuffles=0
        Merged Map outputs=2
```

Figure 3.5. MapReduce Job Counters and Framework Details in the Execution Log

5. Verify output.

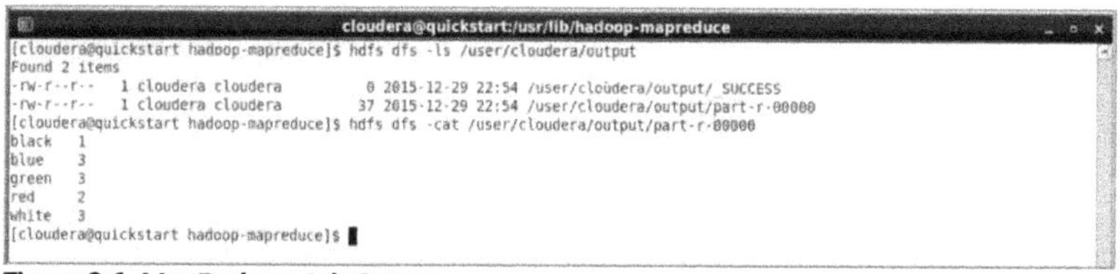

```
                cloudera@quickstart:/usr/lib/hadoop-mapreduce
[cloudera@quickstart hadoop-mapreduce]$ hdfs dfs -ls /user/cloudera/output
Found 2 items
-rw-r--r--   1 cloudera cloudera          0 2015-12-29 22:54 /user/cloudera/output/_SUCCESS
-rw-r--r--   1 cloudera cloudera         37 2015-12-29 22:54 /user/cloudera/output/part-r-00000
[cloudera@quickstart hadoop-mapreduce]$ hdfs dfs -cat /user/cloudera/output/part-r-00000
black   1
blue    3
green   3
red     2
white   3
[cloudera@quickstart hadoop-mapreduce]$
```

Figure 3.6. MapReduce Job Output

CHAPTER 4
MAPREDUCE PROGRAMMING

In this chapter, we will see how to develop a MapReduce program using eclipse as the development environment.

4.1 USE CASE

The dataset used is the MovieLens 1M Dataset [17] provided by GroupLens Research. The dataset is obtained by GroupLens from MovieLens, a movie recommendation website. This data set contains 10000054 ratings and 95580 tags applied to 10681 movies by 71567 users in three files, movies.dat, ratings.dat and tags.dat.

Movies.dat files contains movie information with format MovieID::Title::Genres (sample row: 1356::Star Trek: First Contact (1996)::Action|Adventure|Sci-Fi). Ratings.dat file contains movie rating given by users with format UserID::MovieID::Rating::Timestamp (sample row: 2::647::3::978299351).

We will develop a MapReduce application to find the average movie rating using rating.dat file.

- First copy the input files to HDFS.

```
cloudera@quickstart ~]$ hdfs dfs –mkdir /user/cloudera/input

[cloudera@quickstart ~]$ hdfs dfs -copyFromLocal /home/cloudera/Desktop/ratings.dat /user/cloudera/input
```

- In the Cloudera VM, open eclipse. Create a new java project. Add dependencies jars. Right click on the project -> Build Path -> Configure Build Path. On Libraries tab, select Add External Jars. Browse and add the jars under /usr/lib/Hadoop/client-0.20.

4.2 SOURCE CODE

```java
// MovieAvgRating.java import
java.io.IOException;

import org.apache.hadoop.conf.Configuration; import
org.apache.hadoop.fs.Path;

import org.apache.hadoop.io.FloatWritable; import
org.apache.hadoop.io.IntWritable; import
org.apache.hadoop.io.LongWritable; import
org.apache.hadoop.io.Text;

import org.apache.hadoop.mapreduce.Job; import
org.apache.hadoop.mapreduce.Mapper; import
org.apache.hadoop.mapreduce.Reducer;

import org.apache.hadoop.mapreduce.lib.input.FileInputFormat; import
org.apache.hadoop.mapreduce.lib.output.FileOutputFormat; public class
MovieAvgRating {
        public static class Map extends
                        Mapper<LongWritable, Text, Text, IntWritable> {
                public void map(LongWritable key, Text value, Context context) throws IOException,
                                InterruptedException {
                        String[] tokens = value.toString().split("::"); String movie =
                        tokens[1];
                        int rating = Integer.parseInt(tokens[2]); context.write(new Text(movie), new
                        IntWritable(rating));
                }
        }
        public static class Reduce extends
                        Reducer<Text, IntWritable, Text, FloatWritable> { public void
                reduce(Text key, Iterable<IntWritable> values,
                                Context context) throws IOException, InterruptedException { int counter = 0; int
                        sum = 0;
                        for (IntWritable val : values) { sum +=
                                val.get(); counter++;
                        }
                        float avg = sum / counter; context.write(key, new
                        FloatWritable(avg));
                }
        }
```

```
public static void main(String[] args) throws Exception { Configuration conf =
        new Configuration();
    Job job = Job.getInstance(conf, "movie rating");
    job.setJarByClass(MovieAvgRating.class); job.setMapperClass(Map.class);
    job.setReducerClass(Reduce.class); job.setOutputKeyClass(Text.class);
    job.setMapOutputValueClass(IntWritable.class);
    job.setOutputValueClass(FloatWritable.class);
    FileInputFormat.addInputPath(job, new Path(args[0]));
    FileOutputFormat.setOutputPath(job, new Path(args[1]));
    System.exit(job.waitForCompletion(true) ? 0 : 1);
    }
}
}
```

A MapReduce application typically implements map and reduce methods of Mapper and Reduce classes, respectively. Here the map method processes the input file line by line, splits the lines based on the given delimiter "::" and creates the mapper output key-value pair as (MovieID, Rating). The reduce method calculates the average of values (ratings) for each key (MovieID) and gives the output key-value pair (MovieID, Average Rating).

It is important to give the correct types for input and output key-value pairs. For example, since the average rating calculated is a float value, the type of output value of Reduce method is given as FloatWritable.

In the main method, the MapReduce job configuration is created via Job instance. Mapper, Reducer, key/value types, input files and output paths can be configured in a Job. job.waitForCompletion submits the job and monitors its progress.

4.3 EXECUTION

1. For debugging, the program can be executed in eclipse using a sample input file. In this case, Hadoop runs in LocalJobRunner mode, where all daemons

run in a single JVM. The built-in debug features of eclipse can be handy at this stage. Also, the input and output files will be in local file path, not HDFS.

2. Create a sample input file data.txt with a few lines of data from ratings.dat within the project folder.

3. Next create a Run Configuration for the application. Go to Run -> Run Configuration -> Java Application, right click and select New. In the arguments tab, enter the input file data.txt and name of output folder which will be created inside the project folder for the program output. Click on Run and verify the output.

4. To run the program in the cluster mode, the project needs to be exported into a jar file. Right click on the project and select Export. Select Java -> Jar File -> Enter the export destination (say home/cloudera/Desktop/movierating.jar) -> Next -> Next. For 'Select the class of the application entry point', click on Browse and select the class name MovieAvgRating and click on Finish.

5. On the terminal, go to Desktop and enter the following command to execute the MapReduce application.

---

cloudera@quickstart ~]$ hadoop jar movierating.jar /user/cloudera/input/ratings.dat /user/cloudera/output

Figure 4.1. Executing MapReduce Application

If the application entry point was not set with the class name in the jar, the main class

name needs to be specified during the execution as below:

```
cloudera@quickstart ~]$ hadoop jar movierating.jar MovieAvgRating
/user/cloudera/data/rating.dat /user/cloudera/output
```

6. Verify output.

```
[cloudera@quickstart ~]$ hdfs dfs -ls /user/cloudera/output
Found 2 items
-rw-r--r--      1 cloudera cloudera          0     2016-01-31  00:13
/user/cloudera/output/_SUCCESS
-rw-r--r--      1 cloudera cloudera      32221     2016-01-31  00:13
/user/cloudera/output/part-r-00000
[cloudera@quickstart ~]$ hdfs dfs -cat /user/cloudera/output/part-r-00000
```

Figure 4.2. Displaying the Output File

7. Output can be copied from HDFS to local file path and opened in a file editor or shared as needed.

```
[cloudera@quickstart ~]$ hdfs dfs –copyToLocal /user/cloudera/output/ part-r-00000
/home/cloudera/Desktop
```

CHAPTER 5

DATA ANALYSIS USING APACHE PIG

Pig [18] is a data analysis platform for big data which runs on top of Hadoop. Pig uses a procedural language called Pig Latin and Pig compiler converts it into a sequence of MapReduce jobs. Pig allows the user to perform complex data analysis easily without the need to write the equivalent MapReduce programs in Java.

5.1 EXECUTION MODES

Pig can be run either in interactive mode or batch mode. To run in interactive mode, invoke Grunt shell using 'pig' command and then enter the Pig commands and statements interactively in the Grunt shell. Pig can be run in batch mode using Pig scripts. Pig script is a group of Pig commands and statements put into a single file. The pig script files usually use .pig extension, though it is not mandatory.

Interactive mode or batch mode can be run either in local or MapReduce mode. In local mode, there is no distributed execution; rather it uses the local host and file system where Pig is running.

$ pig -x local

In MapReduce mode, which is the default mode, the execution is done in a distributed fashion on the Hadoop cluster.

$ pig Or $ pig -x mapreduce

5.2 USING PIG FOR DATA ANALYSIS

The dataset used is the MovieLens 1M Dataset [14] mentioned earlier in chapter 4. We will write a pig script to compute the average movie rating using movies.dat and ratings.dat files.

1. PigStorage, the built-in default load function is used here to load the input files. Since it takes only a single character as field delimiter, we are doing a simple preprocessing of input files to change the delimiter form '::' to ':'. (Another option would be to write a user-defined load function to load input in a specific format.)

   $ sed -i 's/::/:/g' movies.dat ratings.dat

2. Copy the input files to HDFS.

```
cloudera@quickstart ~]$ hdfs dfs -mkdir /user/cloudera/data

cloudera@quickstart ~]$ hdfs dfs -copyFromLocal /home/cloudera/Desktop/movies.dat /user/cloudera/data

cloudera@quickstart ~]$ hdfs dfs -copyFromLocal /home/cloudera/Desktop/ratings.dat /user/cloudera/data
```

3. Create a pig script, named MovieRatings.pig, as below.

```
-    Load movies.dat
movies = LOAD '/user/cloudera/data/movies.dat' USING PigStorage(':') As (MovieID:chararray,
Title:chararray, Genres:chararray);

– Load ratings.dat
ratings = LOAD '/user/cloudera/data/ratings.dat' USING PigStorage(':') AS (UserID:chararray,
MovieID:chararray, Rating:float, Timestamp:chararray);

-    Group by MovieID and compute average rating per movie grp_movies =
GROUP ratings by (MovieID);
avg_rating   =   FOREACH   grp_movies   GENERATE   group   as   MovieID,
ROUND(AVG(ratings.Rating)*100.0)/100.0 as Avg_Rating;

-    Join average ratings and movies based on MovieID to map the movie title to the average rating
join_movies_avg_rating = JOIN movies by MovieID, avg_rating by MovieID;

-    Generate the final output and sort by average rating
movies_avg_rating = FOREACH join_movies_avg_rating GENERATE $0 as MovieID, $1 as Title, $4 as
Avg_Rating;


movies_avg_rating_sorted = ORDER movies_avg_rating BY Avg_Rating DESC; STORE
movies_avg_rating_sorted INTO '/user/cloudera/pig/out'
```

First, data is loaded from input files using LOAD operator to form relations 'movies' and 'ratings'. Ratings are grouped by MovieID using GROUP operator and the average rating is then calculated for each Movie. Relations movies and avg_rating are joined based on the common field MovieID using JOIN operator so that movie title from movies relation can be mapped to the average rating from avg_rating relation. Final output is generated by picking the columns MovieID, Title and Avg_Rating. Output is sorted in descending order of average rating. STORE command is used to save the final output on HDFS.

4. Execute the pig script.

```
$ pig MovieRating.pig
```

```
                                          cloudera@quickstart:~                                    _ □ ×
File  Edit  View  Search  Terminal  Help
HadoopVersion   PigVersion    UserId  StartedAt        FinishedAt        Features
2.6.0-cdh5.5.0  0.12.0-cdh5.5.0 cloudera   2016-01-01 23:37:38   2016-01-01 23:40:10   HASH_JOIN,GROUP_BY,ORDER_BY

Success!

Job Stats (time in seconds):
JobId    Maps    Reduces MaxMapTime      MinMapTime    AvgMapTime      MedianMapTime  MaxReduceTime  MinReduceTime  AvgReduc
eTime    MedianReducetime    Alias  Feature Outputs
job_1450421134661_0064  1      1      13      13      13      13      7      7      7      7      avg_rating,grp_movies,ra
tings   GROUP_BY,COMBINER
job_1450421134661_0065  2      1      12      11      12      12      8      8      8      8      join_movies_avg_rating,m
ovies,movies_avg_rating HASH_JOIN
job_1450421134661_0066  1      1      5       5       5       5       6      6      6      6      movies_avg_rating_sorted
SAMPLER
job_1450421134661_0067  1      1      5       5       5       5       6      6      6      6      movies_avg_rating_sorted
ORDER_BY     /user/cloudera/pig/out,

Input(s):
Successfully read 1000209 records (21593884 bytes) from: "/user/cloudera/pig/ratings.dat"
Successfully read 3883 records from: "/user/cloudera/pig/movies.dat"

Output(s):
Successfully stored 3706 records (123578 bytes) in: "/user/cloudera/pig/out"

Counters:
Total records written : 3706
Total bytes written : 123578
Spillable Memory Manager spill count : 0
Total bags proactively spilled: 0
Total records proactively spilled: 0
```

Figure 5.1. Execution Logs on the Console

5. Verify output.

```
[cloudera@quickstart ~]$ hdfs dfs -ls /user/cloudera/pig/out Found 2 items
-rw-r--r--      1 cloudera cloudera              0    2016-01-31  23:40
/user/cloudera/pig/out/_SUCCESS
-rw-r--r--      1 cloudera cloudera          32221    2016-01-31  23:40
/user/cloudera/pig/out/part-r-00000
[cloudera@quickstart ~]$ hdfs dfs -cat /user/cloudera/pig/out/part-r-00000
```

```
                                    cloudera@quickstart:~                            _ □ x
File  Edit  View  Search  Terminal  Help
138       Neon Bible, The (1995)   2.5
1773      Tokyo Fist (1995)        2.5
1782      Little City (1998)       2.5
2242      Grandview, U.S.A. (1984)        2.5
2200      Under Capricorn (1949)   2.5
3592      Time Masters (Les Maîtres du Temps) (1982)      2.5
585       North (1994)     2.49
132       Jade (1995)      2.49
3579      I Dreamed of Africa (2000)      2.49
1592      Air Bud (1997)   2.49
2386      Holy Man (1998) 2.49
2373      Red Sonja (1985)        2.48
3453      Here on Earth (2000)    2.48
19        Ace Ventura     2.48
1887      Almost Heroes (1998)    2.48
2458      Armed and Dangerous (1986)      2.48
1359      Jingle All the Way (1996)       2.48
3162      Simpatico (1999)        2.48
415       Another Stakeout (1993) 2.48
2992      Rawhead Rex (1986)      2.48
3004      Bachelor, The (1999)    2.48
447       Favor, The (1994)       2.48
191       Scarlet Letter, The (1995)      2.47
489       Made in America (1993)  2.47
1520      Commandments (1997)     2.47
611       Hellraiser      2.47
3626      8 1/2 Women (1999)      2.47
```

Figure 5.2. Pig Script Output (Column 1: MovieID, Column 2: Title, Column 3: Average Rating)

6. DUMP command is useful for debugging. DUMP, unlike STORE, will not store the results persistently in the file system; rather it will display the results on the screen. You can create a relation and then 'DUMP' it to verify the correctness of the result.

For example, *DUMP avg_rating* will give the result below:

```
                                    cloudera@quickstart:~                            _ □ x
File  Edit  View  Search  Terminal  Help
(3431,2.67)
(3432,2.26)
(3433,2.15)
(3434,2.26)
(3435,4.42)
(3436,2.79)
(3437,2.0)
(3438,2.68)
(3439,2.13)
(3440,1.92)
(3441,3.28)
(3442,2.31)
(3443,3.0)
(3444,3.23)
(3445,3.19)
(3446,3.41)
(3447,3.72)
(3448,3.73)
(3449,2.97)
(3450,3.42)
(3451,3.92)
(3452,3.14)
(3453,2.48)
(3454,2.7)
(3456,3.94)
(3457,2.99)
(3458,3.0)
```

Figure 5.3. Output of DUMP avg_rating

7. DESCRIBE is another useful operator. It is useful to understand the schema of a relation. For example, *DESCRIBE join_movie_avg_rating* will display the schema as:

join_movie_avg_rating: {movie::MovieID: chararray, movie::Title: chararray, movie::Genres: chararray, avg_rating::MovieID: chararray, avg_rating::Avg_Rating: double}

5.3 USING PIG EDITOR IN HUE

Hue [19] provides a user friendly web interface for data analysis using Hadoop. Open

Hue interface (http://quickstart.cloudera:8888/). If prompted for user/password, enter

cloudera/cloudera.

1. Choose Query Editors -> Pig. 'Editor' screen is displayed. Previously created scripts can be managed from 'Scripts' screen. Previously executed jobs can be viewed on Dashboard screen.

Figure 5.4. Pig Editor in Hue

2. Click on New Script on the left panel, create the script and save it by giving a name.

Figure 5.5. Creating a Pig Script in Hue

3. Execute the script by clicking Submit. The progress bar is displayed showing the percentage of progress along with the execution logs.

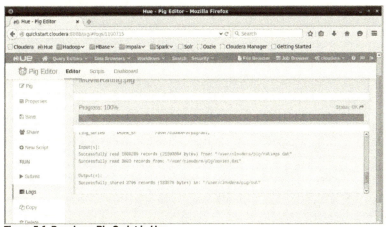

Figure 5.6. Running a Pig Script in Hue

4. To view the output, either click on the output folder link in the log or navigate to the output folder using File Browser application. File Browser

lets you manage the

HDFS. By default, the output file is displayed as binary. Click on 'View as text' button under ACTIONS and the output is displayed as shown below.

Figure 5.7. Displaying Pig Script Output in Hue

CHAPTER 6

DATA ANALYSIS USING APACHE HIVE

Apache Hive is another popular data processing platform built on top of Hadoop. Hive uses a query language HiveQL, which is very similar to SQL. The queries are converted to a series of MapReduce jobs.

Users interact with Hive through a command-line interface called Hive shell, which can be invoked by 'hive' command.

```
% hive
hive>
```

The user can execute the commands in interactive mode by typing in the commands in the Hive shell. Commands must be terminated by a semicolon. To run Hive queries in a batch/non-interactive mode, invoke Hive shell using −e or −f option.

```
$ hive −f <file path>
```

This will execute the queries mentioned in the specified file.

```
$ hive −e '<query 1; ... query n;>';
```

-e option is used to specify the queries inline.

6.1 USING HIVE FOR DATA ANALYSIS

Let us solve the same problem of finding the average movie rating that was discussed in the earlier chapters.

1. The command below lists all the hive databases. Default database can be referred to by 'default'.

```
hive> SHOW DATABASES;
```

2. Create a database.

```
hive> CREATE DATABASE movie_analytics;
```

```
hive> use movie_analytics;
```

The specified database will be used for all subsequent commands.

3. Create 'movies' table with three columns MovieID (integer), Title (string) and Genres
(string). ROW FORMAT here says the files in arrow are delimited by the character
':'. The data will be stored as plain text file. TEXTFILE is the default file storage format.

```
hive> CREATE TABLE movies (MovieID INT, Title STRING, Genres STRING) ROW FORMAT
DELIMITED FIELDS TERMINATED BY ':'
STORED AS TEXTFILE;
```

Similarly create a table for
4. ratings.

```
hive> CREATE TABLE ratings (UserID INT,                MovieID STRING, Rating FLOAT, Timestamp
STRING)
ROW FORMAT DELIMITED FIELDS TERMINATED BY            ':'
STORED AS TEXTFILE;
```

5. Verify the table columns using DESCRIBE statement

```
hive> DESCRIBE movies; hive>
DESCRIBE ratings;
```

6. Now load the data stored earlier on HDFS into these tables. (The data files were stored on HDFS in the directory /user/cloudera/data/ during the analysis using pig.)

```
hive> LOAD DATA INPATH '/user/cloudera/data/movies.dat' OVERWRITE INTO TABLE movies; hive> LOAD DATA
INPATH '/user/cloudera/data/ratings.dat' OVERWRITE INTO TABLE ratings;
```

6.1. Files can be loaded from local filesystem using LOCAL keyword as below:

```
hive> LOAD DATA LOCAL INPATH '/home/cloudera/Desktop/movies.dat' OVERWRITE INTO TABLE movies;
```

6.2. LOAD command puts the specified files in Hive's warehouse directory which is set by the hive.metastore.warehouse.dir property which defaults to /user/hive/warehouse.

To display the property value:

```
hive > SET hive.metastore.warehouse.dir
```

movies.dat   and   ratings.dat   are   copied   to

/user/hive/warehouse/movies_analytics.db directory.

6.3. Hive follows 'schema on read.' During load operation, data is not verified against the table schema. Data files are simply copied to the Hive directory, which makes loading data very fast. The schema is verified only during query operations.

6.4. The actual data is thus stored in HDFS. The table metadata is stored in a relational database. Hive uses an embedded Derby database by default, which runs in the same process as the main Hive service. It can be configured to use a standalone database which is JDBC compliant like MySQL for metadata storage.

7. Verify the table content using SELECT statement.

```
hive> SELECT * from movies;

hive> SELECT * from ratings;
```

8. Find the average movie ratings from the ratings table and join it with movies table to map the movie details with average rating. The output is displayed in the ascending order of average rating.

```
hive> SELECT a.MovieID , a.Title, b.avg_rating from movies a
JOIN (SELECT MovieID , avg(Rating) avg_rating FROM ratings GROUP BY MovieID ) b ON (a.MovieID =
b.MovieID )
SORT BY avg_rating ASC;
```

Figure 6.1. Hive Query Execution

47

```
cloudera@quickstart:~/Desktop
File  Edit  View  Search  Terminal  Help
2004    Christmas Story, A (1983)       4.23290532544(78)
930     Thin Man, The (1934)    4.239720627997261
3466    Hustler, The (1961)     4.24
954     Mr. Smith Goes to Washington (1939)     4.240268877284595
1260    Apocalypse Now (1979)  4.24319727091564
670     Some Folks Call It a Slang Blade (1993) 4.24589803921560
1247    Graduate, The (1967)    4.245036037584215
919     Wizard of Oz, The (1939)        4.247962747308675
1208    Killing Fields, The (1984)      4.24863387978142
951     His Girl Friday (1940)  4.24937027770706
3730    Conversation, The (1974)        4.249440123629309
214     Before the Rain (Pred dozhdot) (1994)   4.25
1002    Ed's Next Move (1996)   4.25
1117    Eighth Day, The (Le Huitième jour ) (1996)      4.25
596     Window to Paris (1994)  4.25
1278    Young Frankenstein (1974)       4.256620607225482
969     African Queen, The (1951)       4.25165562913907
1225    Amadeus (1984)  4.251060972503618
1189    Thin Blue Line, The (1988)      4.25278018408022
1276    Cool Hand Luke (1967)   4.253763446066215
3604    Seven Days in May (1964)        4.254543454545455
668     Fargo (1996)    4.25407360048501
926     All About Eve (1950)    4.25558132653060068
363     Wonderful, Horrible Life of Leni Riefenstahl, The (Die Macht der Bilder) (1993) 4.258064516129032
1132    Manon of the Spring (Manon des sources) (1986)  4.25969090909090
1272    Patton (1970)   4.26066606666667
1217    Ran (1985)      4.268967503025251
1045    On the Waterfront (1954)        4.26974951830443I
2203    Shadow of a Doubt (1943)        4.270306266054205
903     Vertigo (1958)  4.27292017679558
541     Blade Runner (1982)     4.27733333333333
3679    Decline of Western Civilization, The (1981)     4.274193540347097
1213    GoodFellas (1990)       4.275196137950049
298     Pulp Fiction (1994)     4.27621e05159913
1469    Inherit the Wind (1960) 4.27905074620056
905     It Happened One Night (1934)    4.28074066038161004
899     Singin' in the Rain (1952)      4.28362183758499335
3091    Kagemusha (1980)        4.283667943262412
2357    Central Station (Central do Brasil) (1998)      4.2837209303232558
1224    Henry V (1989)  4.2863049567252622
1172    Cinema Paradiso (1998)  4.287904670048701
2937    Palm Beach Story, The (1942)    4.280461530401538
1254    Treasure of the Sierra Madre, The (1948)        4.209103222958050
1198    Star Wars       4.29297050862763
930     Notorious (1946)        4.29438202247191
1203    12 Angry Men (1957)     4.295454545454546
953     It's a Wonderful Life (1946)    4.299939700051262
2931    Time of the Gypsies (Dom za vesanje) (1989)     4.3
2839    West Beirut (West Beyrouth) (1998)      4.3
910     Some Like It Hot (1959) 4.300400703230769
898     Philadelphia Story, The (1940)  4.30008720832233675
1260    M (1931)        4.301940051040515
3233    Boot, The (Das Boot) (1981)     4.30265736269733I
1197    Princess Bride, The (1987)      4.30171005490944045
2106    Strangers on a Train (1951)     4.30497925311261I
2398    Celebration, The (Festen) (1998)        4.3076923070923075
1284    Big Sleep, The (1946)   4.31230447319770I
2571    Matrix, The (1999)      4.31503613030110
```

Figure 6.2. Hive Query Output

48

CHAPTER 7
BIG DATA ANALYTICS ON AMAZON CLOUD

7.1 AMAZON WEB SERVICES

Amazon Web Services (AWS) [20] is a cloud computing platform from Amazon. Amazon Elastic Compute Cloud (EC2) provides the computing resources. EC2 provides different instance types with a range of resource combinations to meet different requirements. You can reserve the resources according to your computing requirements and scale them easily. The resource costs are per the actual usage, i.e. for the duration when the servers are up and running. Amazon Elastic MapReduce (EMR) is basically the Hadoop framework running on cloud. Amazon Simple Storage Service (S3) provides data storage service where bulk input and output data can be stored.

7.2 CREATE AN EMR CLUSTER

Follow the steps below to create an EMR cluster using AWS console [21].

1. Create an AWS account (http://aws.amazon.com/). Some services are free under the Free Tier registration and additional services can be used at applicable rates [22].

Figure 7.1. AWS Console with Available Services

(EC2 under Compute, S3 under Storage & Content Delivery, EMR under Analytics)

2. Go to S3 (Scalable Storage in the Cloud) console at https://console.aws.amazon.com/s3/ and create an S3 Bucket and folders for data and log files.

3. Create an Amazon EC2 key pair which is required to connect to the nodes in the cluster over Secure Shell (SSH) protocol later.

Go to Amazon EC2 console at https://console.aws.amazon.com/ec2/ and select NETWORK & SECURITY -> Key Pairs. Create a key pair and download the private key file (.pem format).

4. Go to Amazon EMR console at https://console.aws.amazon.com/elasticmapreduce/ and create
a cluster.

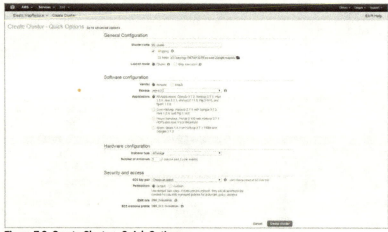

Figure 7.2. Create Cluster - Quick Options

5. Click on Go to advanced options for a detailed view.

6. Go with the default Software Configuration. By default, Hadoop, Pig, Hive and Hue are selected.

6.1. Steps like Hive program, Pig program, Custom JAR (MapReduce program) etc. can be specified so that these will be executed once the cluster is up.

6.2. Marking the check box 'Auto-terminate cluster after the last step is completed' will create a transient cluster. A transient cluster automatically terminates when all the steps are executed (even if Termination Protection is turned on in the next screen). If auto-termination is disabled, it will create a long-running cluster which persists even after all the steps are executed.

Figure 7.3. Create Cluster - Software Configuration

7. By default, a cluster with one master and two slaves with m3.xlarge (vCPU: 4, Mem (GiB):15) instance type [23] is configured under Hardware Configuration.

Figure 7.4. Create Cluster - Hardware Configuration

8. In General Option screen, select the S3 folder created in step 2 for logging.

Bootstrap Actions can be specified which are setup scripts to be executed before Hadoop starts on each cluster node.

8.1. By default Termination protection is turned on to protect the cluster from termination by accident. This must be disabled before a cluster has to be terminated. When a user terminates a running cluster for which the termination protection was turned on, user will be prompted to turn off the termination protection before the cluster can be terminated.

Figure 7.5. Create Cluster - General Options

9. In Security Options screen, choose the EC2 key pair created in step 3.

Figure 7.6. Create Cluster - Security Options

10. Click on Create Cluster. Cluster will be in Starting state while the EC2 instances are being provisioned.

Figure 7.7. Cluster in Starting State

11. If Steps were specified, those will be executed in order. Cluster goes into Running state while processing the steps. If auto-termination was on, the cluster will be terminated after the steps are completed, or the cluster will go into Waiting state.

Figure 7.8. Cluster in Waiting State

7.3 CONNECT TO THE MASTER NODE

To connect to the master node of the cluster using PuTTY, an SSH client, on Windows:

1. PuTTY needs private key in .ppk format.

    1.1. Use PuTTYgen to convert the private key .pem file stored earlier to .ppk format.

Figure 7.9. PuTTYgen

    1.2. Select SSH-2 RSA for the type of key to generate. Click on Load and select All Files (*.*) and select the .pem file. Click OK in the pop up.

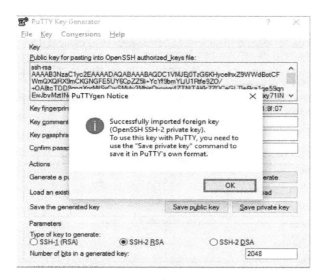

Figure 7.10. Converting Private Key to .ppk Format

1.3. Save the private key in .ppk format by clicking 'Save private key'.

2. Open PuTTY. For Host Name, enter hadoop@<Public DNS name of Master node>. Public DNS name of Master node can be obtained by going to the cluster in Amazon EMR console.

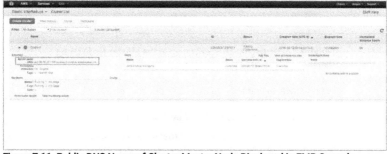

Figure 7.11. Public DNS Name of Cluster Master Node Displayed in EMR Console

3. Select Category -> Connection -> SSH -> Auth and select the .ppk file from step 1 for
'Private key file for authentication'.

4. To view the web interfaces Hosted on the Master Node (as explained in detail in the following section), an SSH Tunnel needs to be set up to the Master Node Using Dynamic Port Forwarding.

4.1. Select Category -> Connection -> SSH ->Tunnels. Enter 8157 (an unused local port) for 'Source port'.

4.2. Leave the Destination field blank. Select Dynamic and Auto options. Choose
Add.

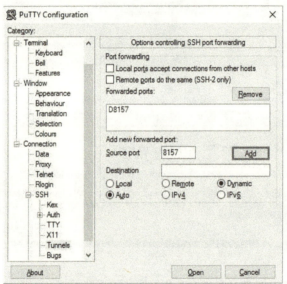

Figure 7.12. Setting up an SSH Tunnel to the Master Node Using Dynamic Port Forwarding

5. Click on 'Open' to connect.

7.4 VIEW WEB INTERFACES HOSTED ON THE MASTER NODE

Web connection needs to be enabled in order to view the web interfaces for Hue, Resource Manager, etc. hosted on the master node. Enable Web Connection link is displayed on the cluster creation page with instructions on how to set up the web connection.

Figure 7.13. Instructions to Setup Web Connection

1. Set up an SSH Tunnel to the Master Node Using Dynamic Port Forwarding by performing step 1 - 4 above for connecting to the Master using PuTTY.

2. Configure Proxy Settings in the browser. To configure FoxyProxy for Chrome:

   - Download and install FoxyProxy Standard from http://getfoxyproxy.org/downloads.html Chrome
   - Restart Chrome
   - Create foxyproxy-settings.xml file containing the following:

```xml
<?xml version="1.0" encoding="UTF-8"?>
<foxyproxy>
    <proxies>
        <proxy name="emr-socks-proxy" id="2322596116" notes="" fromSubscription="false"
enabled="true" mode="manual" selectedTabIndex="2" lastresort="false" animatedIcons="true"
includeInCycle="true" color="#0055E5" proxyDNS="true" noInternalIPs="false" autoconfMode="pac"
clearCacheBeforeUse="false" disableCache="false" clearCookiesBeforeUse="false"
rejectCookies="false">
            <matches>
                <match enabled="true" name="*ec2*.amazonaws.com*"
pattern="*ec2*.amazonaws.com*" isRegEx="false" isBlackList="false" isMultiLine="false"
caseSensitive="false" fromSubscription="false" />
                <match enabled="true" name="*ec2*.compute*" pattern="*ec2*.compute*"
isRegEx="false" isBlackList="false" isMultiLine="false" caseSensitive="false"
fromSubscription="false" />
                <match enabled="true" name="10.*" pattern="http://10.*" isRegEx="false"
isBlackList="false" isMultiLine="false" caseSensitive="false" fromSubscription="false" />
                <match enabled="true" name="*10*.amazonaws.com*"
pattern="*10*.amazonaws.com*" isRegEx="false" isBlackList="false" isMultiLine="false"
caseSensitive="false" fromSubscription="false" />
                <match enabled="true" name="*10*.compute*" pattern="*10*.compute*"
isRegEx="false" isBlackList="false" isMultiLine="false" caseSensitive="false"
fromSubscription="false"/>
                <match enabled="true" name="*.compute.internal*"
pattern="*.compute.internal*" isRegEx="false" isBlackList="false" isMultiLine="false"
caseSensitive="false" fromSubscription="false"/>
                <match enabled="true" name="*.ec2.internal*" pattern="*.ec2.internal*"
isRegEx="false" isBlackList="false" isMultiLine="false" caseSensitive="false"
fromSubscription="false"/>
            </matches>
            <manualconf host="localhost" port="8157" socksversion="5" isSocks="true"
username="" password="" domain="" />
        </proxy>
    </proxies>
</foxyproxy>
```

- Open Chrome and click on Firefox icon on the toolbar and choose Options.

- Select Import/Export. Click Choose File, select foxyproxy-settings.xml, and click Open. In the Import FoxyProxy Settings dialog, click Add.

- For Proxy mode, choose Use proxies based on their pre-defined patterns and priorities.

- Now that the web connection set up is done, on the Cluster Details screen, active links for the web interfaces hosted on the cluster will be displayed (Click on the cluster name in the cluster list in EMR to go to the Cluster Details screen.)

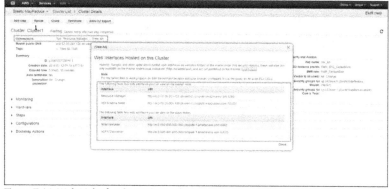

Figure 7.14. Web Links for the Web Interfaces Hosted on the Cluster

7.5 SUBMIT A JOB TO THE CLUSTER

To submit a job to a running cluster:

1. Upload the jar file and input file to S3.

Figure 7.15. Upload MapReduce Program Jar File to S3

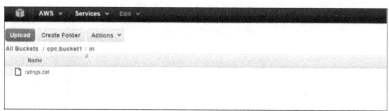

Figure 7.16. Upload Input File to S3

2. Go to the cluster in the Cluster List in Elastic MapReduce console and click on Add Step.

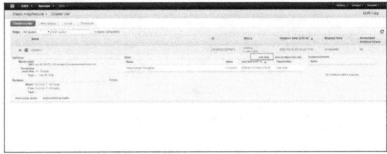

Figure 7.17. Add Step to a Running Cluster

3. Provide the jar location in S3 and input and output path as arguments. Make sure output path given does not exist already. If the class of the application entry point was not specified while exporting the jar (This can be verified by checking if Main-Class was specified in the jar's manifest file), specify the main class as the first argument.

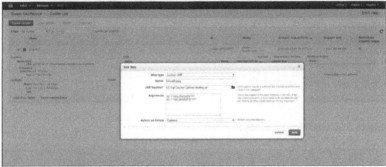

Figure 7.18. Add Step to Execute a Custom Jar File

4. The step will be in Pending state initially. It will then move to Running state and finally to Completed state when the execution is complete. If the step execution fails, it will move to Failed state. Output folder is created and the output can be verified from the S3 console. Logs are generated in the configured S3 logs location and it can be used for debugging failed steps.

Figure 7.19. Output Folder in S3

7.6 Using Hue On Amazon EMR

Go to Hue at http://<public DNS Name of Master>:8888 or by clicking the link for Hue on the Cluster Details screen (Figure 7.14). Give username as hadoop and create a password. Note: Username other than hadoop can also be used. Since the SSH connections uses hadoop user, it is safe to use the same user in hue to avoid file ownership issues.

Figure 7.20. Hue Login Screen

Using Pig Editor in Hue was already explained in chapter 6. In this section, using Hive Editor in Hue to run the Hive queries and using Hue's Metastore Manager to manage Hive metastore are discussed.

7.6.1 Using Hive Editor in Hue

1. Copy input files to the master node using WinSCP

    1.1 Give public DNS name of the master node in Host name and Hadoop as user name. Click on Advanced and under SSH -> Authentication.

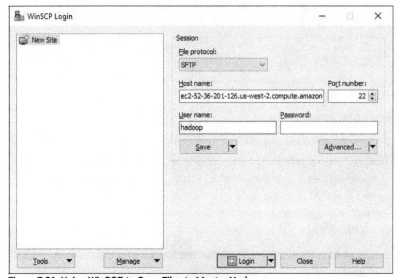

Figure 7.21. Using WinSCP to Copy Files to Master Node

    1.2 Select .ppk generated earlier in the private key file and click Ok. Click on Login.

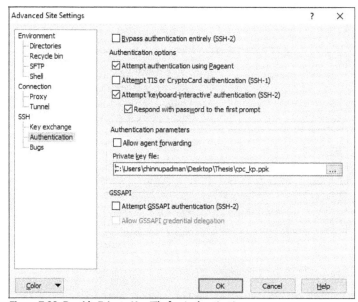

Figure 7.22. Provide Private Key File for Authentication

   1.3 Copy movies.dat and ratings.dat to /home/Hadoop directory.

2. Connect to the master node via PuTTy (section 7.3) and copy these files to HDFS.

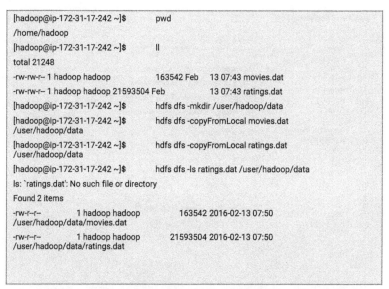

```
[hadoop@ip-172-31-17-242 ~]$        pwd
/home/hadoop
[hadoop@ip-172-31-17-242 ~]$        ll
total 21248
-rw-rw-r-- 1 hadoop hadoop         163542 Feb    13 07:43 movies.dat
-rw-rw-r-- 1 hadoop hadoop 21593504 Feb            13 07:43 ratings.dat
[hadoop@ip-172-31-17-242 ~]$        hdfs dfs -mkdir /user/hadoop/data
[hadoop@ip-172-31-17-242 ~]$        hdfs dfs -copyFromLocal movies.dat
/user/hadoop/data
[hadoop@ip-172-31-17-242 ~]$        hdfs dfs -copyFromLocal ratings.dat
/user/hadoop/data
[hadoop@ip-172-31-17-242 ~]$        hdfs dfs -ls ratings.dat /user/hadoop/data
ls: `ratings.dat': No such file or directory
Found 2 items
-rw-r--r--          1 hadoop hadoop          163542 2016-02-13 07:50
/user/hadoop/data/movies.dat
-rw-r--r--          1 hadoop hadoop          21593504 2016-02-13 07:50
/user/hadoop/data/ratings.dat
```

3. Hive metastore can be managed by MetaStore Manager in Hue. Go to MetaStore Manager. Click on Databases link and select Create a new database named movie_analytics. Give a database name and by default it gets stored in /user/hive/warehouse/database_name or another location in HDFS can be specified.

Figure 7.23. Create Database Using Metastore Manager

4. Select the created database and create tables. A table can be created either from a file or manually. Select the option to create a new table from a file.

Figure 7.24. Create Tables Using Metastore Manager

4.1. Give table name 'movies' and input file path on

HDFS(/user/hadoop/data/movies.dat) from where the table definition is to be used and data is to be imported. Keep the checkbox for 'Import data from file' checked. Note the warning that the selected file is going to be moved during the import.

Figure 7.25. Create a New Table From a File - Choose File

4.2. Tables can be imported from HDFS to a database stored in HDFS. For example, the database movie_analytics megastore exists in HDFS (in /user/hive/warehouse/ movie_analytics.db). The procedure is different to import a table from Amazon S3 [24].

4.3. Specify the delimiter as ":" and the table data can be previewed to verify the correctness.

Figure 7.26. Create a New Table From a File - Choose Delimiter

4.4. Specify column names and column type.

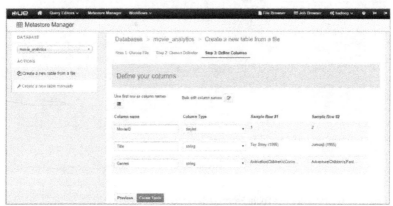

Figure 7.27. Create a New Table From a File - Define Columns

4.5. Click create table. Table gets created and data is imported.

Select the table movies under the database movie_analytics. The schema can be verified under the Columns tab. Verify if the data is imported successfully by checking Sample tab which displays sample rows of the table.

4.6 Similarly, create table 'ratings' from the file on HDFS /user/hadoop/data/ratings.dat.

Figure 7.28. 'ratings' Table Created

5. To run the Hive queries, go to Hive Editor by selecting Query Editors -> Hive. 'Editor' screen is displayed.

6. Select the database from the DATABSE drop down. (Click the refresh button if the newly created database is not listed.)

7. In the editor, enter single or multiple queries and click Execute.

For example, type in "select * from movies". The result is displayed under Results tab.

Figure 7.29. Executing a Hive Query

8. Queries can be saved and later accessed from 'Saved Queries' tab. 'My Queries' tab will show recent saved and run queries.

9. Execute below query to calculate the average movie rating:

```
SELECT a.MovieID , a.Title, b.avg_rating from movies a
JOIN (SELECT MovieID , avg(Rating) avg_rating FROM ratings GROUP BY MovieID )
ON (a.MovieID  = b.MovieID )
```

10. The result can be exported to xls/csv or saved to HDFS or a new hive table.
Logs can be viewed from Logs tab. The results can be viewed in different
chart formats (Bars, Lines, Pie, and Map) in the Chart tab.

Figure 7.30. Hive Query and Result to Calculate Average Movie Rating

CHAPTER 8
FUTURE WORK

We live in a data flooded age. More organizations are becoming aware of the need to analyze their data to get insights, increase efficiency, derive competitive advantage and create new business dimensions. As the need to create value from large volumes of data increases, so do the technologies to store and process such data. There is an increased demand in the market for efficient and cost effective big data technologies as more industries seek these for their data analytical needs.

Apache Hadoop is a popular open source big data framework for distributed data storage and processing. We saw how HDFS and MapReduce, the two core components of Hadoop, enable data storage and data processing of big data. There are a number of supporting tools built around Hadoop's core components, which together form the 'Hadoop Ecosystem' and aid in data analysis, data transfer, scheduling, monitoring, performance and visualization. We saw how Pig and Hive, two data analytical platforms built around Hadoop, enable big data analysis. The main advantage of Pig and Hive is that they abstract data processing from the underlying MapReduce. Writing multi stage map and reduce functions to perform complex data processing tasks in MapReduce can be difficult and time consuming. High-level frameworks like Pig and Hive provide ease of programming with their powerful abstracted built-in capabilities. For example, we saw the ease of using the join operation in Pig and Hive to join data from two data sets. Writing MapReduce code to perform join operations would be more challenging and time consuming. Pig and Hive also provide capabilities to integrate user defined functions for specific processing needs.

Since both Pig and Hive aid in analysis of large volumes of data, these are often compared against each other to see which is best in specific scenarios. Pig is suitable for data preparation needs like ETL (Extract Transform Load) tasks, whereas Hive is widely used for data warehousing/analysis needs [25]. Pig is comparatively more efficient than Hive for complex queries with lots of joins and filters. Another difference is the type of data that these tools can process efficiently. Hive is efficient for structured data, whereas Pig handles both structured and unstructured data efficiently. Hive is easy to use for developers who are already familiar with SQL queries since HiveQL, Hive's query language, is very SQL-like. Users who are new to Pig Latin, the data-flow language used by Pig, would need to be familiarized with the language initially.

There are other Hadoop related projects such as Apache Spark, Apache HBase, Apache Sqoop, Apache Flume, Apache Zookeeper and Apache Oozie. Spark is a distributed computing engine for fast large-scale data processing. Instead of the MapReduce execution engine, it uses its own runtime engine. Spark runs programs up to 100x faster than Hadoop MapReduce in memory, or 10x faster on disk [26], which makes it suitable for low-latency applications. In MapReduce, data is always loaded from disk, whereas Spark uses in-memory caching to store datasets in memory in between jobs. This makes Spark more efficient for iterative tasks where the operations need to be repeated on a data set. HBase is a distributed, non-relational database built on top of HDFS to provide random, real -time read/write access to big data [27]. It was inspired from Google's BigTable [28]. Sqoop is a tool used for transferring data between Hadoop and relational databases [29]. Flume is used as a log aggregator for collecting large log data from multiple sources and moving to a centralized location [30]. Zookeeper provides centralized coordination services for managing and monitoring large distributed systems [31]. Oozie is a workflow scheduler system to manage Hadoop jobs [32]. It would be interesting to explore the features and use cases of these supporting big data tools to see how these technologies fit together to form the larger ecosystem for efficient storage, processing, and analysis of big data.

REFERENCES

[1] M. CAFARELLA AND D. CUTTING, *Building nutch: Open source search*, ACM Queue, 2 (2004), pp. 1-7.

[2] S. GHEMAWAT, H. GOBIOFF, AND S.-T. LEUNG, *The Google file system*, Symposium on Operating Systems Principles, New York, 2003, Association for Computing Machinery.

[3] J. DEAN AND S. GHEMAWAT, *MapReduce: Simplified data processing on large clusters*, 6th Symposium on Operating Systems Design & Implementation, San Francisco, California, 2004, USENIX.

[4] HADOOP ILLUMINATED, *Chapter 10. Hadoop Use Cases and Case Studies*. Hadoop Illuminated, http://hadoopilluminated.com/hadoop_illuminated/Hadoop_Use_Cases.html, accessed March 2016, n.d.

[5] APACHE HADOOP, *Powered By*. Hadoop Wiki, http://wiki.apache.org/hadoop/PoweredBy, accessed March 2016, n.d.

[6] APACHE HADOOP, *HDFS architecture*. The Apache Software Foundation, http://hadoop. apache.org/docs/current/hadoop-project-dist/hadoop-hdfs/HdfsDesign.html, accessed March 2016, n.d.

[7] R. CHANSLER, H. KUANG, S. RADIA, K. SHVACHKO, AND S. SRINIVAS, *The Hadoop distributed file system*. The Architecture of Open Source Applications, http://www.aosabook.org/en/hdfs.html, accessed March 2016, n.d.

[8] T. WHITE, *Hadoop: The Definitive Guide*. O'Reilly Media, Inc., Sebastopol, California, 2015.

[9] APACHE HADOOP, *MapReduce tutorial*. The Apache Software Foundation, http://hadoop. apache.org/docs/current/hadoop-mapreduce-client/hadoop-mapreduce-client-core/ MapReduceTutorial.html, accessed March 2016, n.d.

[10] APACHE HADOOP, *Apache Hadoop YARN*. The Apache Software Foundation, http://hadoop.apache.org/docs/current/hadoop-yarn/hadoop-yarn-site/YARN.html, accessed March 2016, n.d.

[11] S. BARDHAN AND D. A. MENASCE, *The Anatomy of MapReduce Jobs, Scheduling, and Performance Challenges*, Conf. of the Computer Measurement Group, San Diego, California, November 2013.

[12] APACHE HADOOP, *Products that include Apache Hadoop or derivative works and commercial support*. Hadoop Wiki, https://wiki.apache.org/hadoop/Distributions %20and%20Commercial%20Support, accessed March 2016, n.d.

[13] CLOUDERA'S HADOOP DISTRIBUTION, *Apache Hadoop*. Cloudera, https://www.cloudera. com/products/apache-hadoop.html, accessed March 2016, n.d.

[14] VMWARE, *Download VMware player*. My VMware, https://my.vmware.com/web /vmware/free#desktop_end_user_computing/vmware_player/6_0|PLAYER-607, accessed March 2016, n.d.

[15] CLOUDERA, *QuickStart downloads for CDH 5.5*. Cloudera, http://www.cloudera.com /content/www/en-us/downloads/quickstart_vms/5-5.html, accessed March 2016, n.d.

[16] HADOOP, *HDFS shell commands*. The Apache Software Foundation, http://hadoop. apache.org/docs/current/hadoop-project-dist/hadoop-common/FileSystemShell.html, accessed March 2016, n.d.

[17] GROUPLENS, *MovieLens 1M dataset*. Grouplens, http://grouplens.org/datasets /movielens/1m/, accessed March 2016, n.d.

[18] APACHE, *Welcome to Apache Pig*. Apache, http://pig.apache.org/, accessed March 2016, n.d.

[19] HUE, *Let's big data*. Hue, http://gethue.com/, accessed March 2016, n.d.

[20] AMAZON, *AWS documentation*. Amazon, http://aws.amazon.com/documentation/, accessed March 2016, n.d.

[21] AMAZON, *What is Amazon EMR?*. Amazon, http://docs.aws.amazon.com/ ElasticMapReduce/latest/DeveloperGuide/emr-what-is-emr.html, accessed March 2016, n.d.

[22] AMAZON, *Amazon EC2 pricing*. Amazon, https://aws.amazon.com/ec2/pricing/, accessed March 2016, n.d.

[23] AMAZON, *Amazon EC2 instance types*. Amazon, https://aws.amazon.com/ec2/instance-types/, accessed March 2016, n.d.

[24] AMAZON, *Amazon EMR, Metastore manager restrictions*. Amazon, http://docs.aws. amazon.com/ElasticMapReduce/latest/DeveloperGuide/emr-hue-s3-metastore.html, accessed March 2016, n.d.

[25] ALAN GATES, *Pig and Hive at Yahoo!*. Yahoo, https://developer.yahoo.com/blogs/ hadoop/pig-hive-yahoo-464.html, accessed March 2016, n.d.

[26] APACHE SPARK, *Apache Spark is a fast and general engine for large-scale data processing*. Apache, http://spark.apache.org/, accessed March 2016, n.d.

[27] APACHE HBASE, *Welcome to Apache HBase*. Apache, http://hbase.apache.org/, accessed March 2016, n.d.

[28] F. CHANG, J. DEAN, S. GHEMAWAT, W. C. HSIEH, D. A. WALLACH, M. BURROWS, T. CHANDRA, A. FIKES, AND R. E. GRUBER, *Bigtable: A distributed storage system for structured data*, ACM Trans. on Com. Sys., 26 (2006), pp. 1-26.

[29] APACHE, *Apache Sqoop*. The Apache Software Foundation, http://sqoop.apache.org/, accessed March 2016, n.d.

[30] APACHE FLUME, *Welcome to Apache Flume*. Apache Flume, http://flume.apache.org/, accessed March 2016, n.d.

[31] APACHE ZOOKEPPER, *Welcome to Apache ZooKeeper*. Apache ZooKeeper, http://zookeeper.apache.org/, accessed March 2016, n.d.

[32] APACHE OOZIE, *Apache Oozie workflow scheduler for Hadoop. Apache Oozie*, http://oozie.apache.org/, accessed March 2016, n.d.